NOT JUST A POET

Not Just a Poet

Vol. 1

Poetry in the Rawest Form

ZS Argenio

This is a work of fiction. Names, characters, places, and incidents either are the product of the author's imagination or are used fictitiously. Any resemblance to actual persons, living or dead, events, or locales is entirely coincidental.

Copyright © 2022 by ZS Argenio

All rights reserved. No part of this book may be reproduced or used in any manner without written permission of the copyright owner except for the use of quotations in a book review. For more information, contact: notjustapoet81@gmail.com

First paperback edition: December 2022

ISBNs
978-1-80227-920-7 (Paperback)
978-1-80227-921-4 (eBook)

CONTENTS

Acknowledgement. vii

1. Mental Health 1
    'Promised Story,' 5
    'Suicide' 8
    'The Power of Love,' 10
    Trying.' 12
    'They Say.' 14
    'A Web' 15
    'I wish.' 17
    'Living' 18
    'Dead Head Of Mine' 19
    'Unspoken' 20

2. Love 23
    'The Rose,' 25
    'My Love,' 26
    'My Star,' 28
    'Missed You,' 30

'The Eve Night,' 32

'Our Forever,' 35

'I Spy,' 36

'Your Touch,' 38

'What' 39

'Love And Lust' 41

3. World 43

'Black Lives Matter' 45

'Covid-19' 50

'War,' 52

'Listen,' 55

'Our World'. 57

'The Flower Too The Bee' 58

'Creating' 59

'A Temper From Sour Takes' 60

4. Self Image 63

'Filter' 72

'Courage,' 75

'You Will Make Me Fat' 78

'Mis - Fit' 80

'TV' 82

'My Kingdom' 83

'Look In The Mirror' 85

CONTENTS

'Be Like You' 87
'Image: 88
'Love Yourself' 89

5. Nightmares 91
   'Devil' 93
   'The Gate' 97
   'I Dreamed a Dream, And You Was There' 100
   'Run' 101
   'Asleep or?' 102
   'Am I Awake?' 104
   'Close My Eyes 106

6. Sickness 107
   'Autoimmune' 109
   'Memory,' 111
   'When It Is Hard' 113
   'Anxiety' 115
   'My Diagnosis' 117

7. Family 121
   'My Brother' 123
   'Foster parents' 127
   'To My Sister,' 129
   'Dear Son,' 132

'Grandma's Roasties' 134

'My Grandkids,' 135

'Mummy' 136

'Spontaneous Moments' 138

'Grandchildren A Blessing' 140

'How Many' 142

'My Babies' 143

8. Trauma 145

'It's Happened Before,' 149

'Solitude' 152

'The Street' 154

'Negative,' 157

'Left To Fall' 160

'Your Car' 161

'Face' 164

'Daydream' 165

'Go Away' 166

'Prostitute.' 167

9. letters. 169

'Dear Me,' 170

'Fight For Freedom,' 175

'Searching' 179

'In a Kingdom' 183

CONTENTS

'Can you See Me' 185
'Mine' 188
'The Fulness Of life I Lead' 190
'What Do I Do,' 192
'Feelings' 193
'Dear Toby' 194

Coming Soon 197

ACKNOWLEDGEMENT.

I want to thank my partner for all her help and support in everything I choose to do. My partner's support is so close to my heart due to my not having the best of health. Having her support me in critical areas is something of a kind and is priceless. Through all the bumps in the road, my partner still helped me create this book and continued to support other projects. I really couldn't do this without her.

I would also like to thank my children. As I watch them grow into young adults, they inspire me daily. Watching them succeed in the areas of their life helps me to believe in what I'm doing with my life and my writing. The children all know that writing has always been a part of my life, and I have always wanted to get creative. To have their support means more than the world to me. I also want to thank them for listening to me. They will always humour me and listen when I have yet another piece of poetry or writing to read. I love that so much about them.

My family are my biggest supporters as I am them. I hope to make them all proud with this first book of mine.

Love you all.

BOOKS DO NOT COME WITH AGE RESTRICTIONS, SO I WANT TO WARN YOU THAT THIS BOOK CONTAINS RAW MATERIAL. THEREFORE IS NOT SUITABLE FOR CHILDREN (ADULTS ONLY). THOSE UNDER 18 SHOULD NOT READ WRITINGS TAKEN FROM MY JOURNAL!

CHAPTER 1

Mental Health

(TRIGGER WARNING FOR ALL THIS CHAPTER)

Have you ever felt alone, even though there could be many people surrounding you, yet you cannot see not one of those people? Your eyes are blind, and your ears are deaf to sight and sound. Your mind plays with you and tells you one thing, yet what you understand is entirely different. Your mood can go from high to low in point two of a second. You no longer wish to drag your arse to the shower because the thought seems empty of any pleasure. Why would you want to be clean? Clothes are the same. You have been in your PJs for over two weeks now, with curtains closed and any sign that someone could approach your front door would feel like the ground is going to open up and suck you in; after all, you don't want to see anyone, you don't want to engage in any conversation let alone having to face the postal delivery officer to take in a parcel you stay well away from any food ordering or deliveries that could be possible from the internet, so you're not faced with such agonising tests of speaking one word to anyone.

The thought of your phone ringing is just so mind-bending that it eats you up; the anxiety at this point has grown so much that the ability to answer is so overwhelming that you would instead put your phone in aeroplane mode, hoping no one notices that you are being a recluse. You turn on the television, only to turn it off again, for you get so paranoid that someone can see you via some satellite link or hear you through the television speakers. You pull the plug well and truly out the wall. That's it blinds down, curtains closed and back to bed you go, where you have been living for quite a few dreadful weeks. You are suffering in silence; you have an overwhelming feeling of depression, and it won't shift; it's not that you haven't tried to reach out; you may have sent a subliminal message a few weeks prior, you may have plucked up the courage to call a family member or your well-being team, you feel as though your voice wasn't enough, didn't come across straightforward enough. Now it feels like it's all your fault. You get stuck in a rut, and you find it hard to get out of; it seems inside your head is getting deeper and deeper, and the further down in your mind you get, the worse it is; you try to pull yourself up but you can't; it seems so impossible to you, the easiest of tasks that seemed so long ago are now the hardest of all. As you drag around your blanket, as that seems to be the only safe part of comfort you have right now, you have filled your head with fear, fear of the unknown. But what is that unknown? Everything you once knew feels like it has gone. You look in the mirror and don't even recognise yourself anymore. Then boom, there it is it hits you like a ton of bricks; you don't feel worthy anymore. Any self-esteem you once had is now gone. You have no confidence. The book on courage was also shut down a long time ago, but now you feel you have the answer.

Feeling alone in this world is something that, at some point, we all face in our lives. For some, the obstacle of life, reality and the pain that comes with it are just too much to bear. We find an alternative reality in which we can feel comfortable. One that only exists in our time, the moments that we feel neglected, unloved, and unfulfilled, we look in the mirror, and the reflection we see we hate; the despair is too much. For some of us, there is a way out of the torture we face every waking hour; it's different for everyone who seeks an alternative universe to feel happy, alive and able to meet that day with courage. They found an answer, with an appetite for their freedom, free of everything they felt just two minutes previous. One hit of their new world, a timeline of good versus evil, is now embedded in their brain.

'Promised Story,'

With two mothers, your partner, a family home
your siblings in tow, I struggle to understand why you
feel alone
A happy life with memories you keep
only please remember that what you sow, you reap!
Here is my offer, so explicit, take me as your new life
Now you have met me, take steed, take a knife
For I am your friend, your lover, endure me
I promise you; I will be all that you see
I stand tall and beautiful, like Snow White
I see your aura is so delicately bright
Don't be scared
Go ahead
Cut me and shape me for your friend; I will let you
Can you feel me inside as I'm passing through?
I told you I was helpful. With this courage, you feel
strong
You know me, this can't be wrong!
I beg you to remember
It is only us that belong together
Each time I'm with you, I take hold of that little more
Do you feel me? I'm so exotic and raw
Let me apologise if you are a little sore

This is the only opening that I can enter
for your euphoric rush; I must reach your brain's centre
Please stop your wincing and moaning
I told you I was your friend, so stop groaning!
With me, you must never moan
Without me now, you will be sad and alone!
So keep me, inhale my courage and glory
As promised, I will tell you a story....
I belong to a cult of other whites, some a little dirty
Don't worry, remember around me you are so flirty
I've taken your friends and family too
You even gave me your body, remember you let me through
Once I'm in, I am hard to get out
That's what my personality is all about
The darker your eyes, the more sunken your skin
If you look in the mirror, you will see how much you let me in
You can't run, nor can you hide
In your shadow il be behind
As now you, my friend, belong to me
trust me when I say I will never set you free!
No family or job; without me, you will be alone
STOP IT! I got you this far; don't you dare moan.

MENTAL HEALTH

Tell me, please, is your nose in constant bleeding and pain?
Well, that will be me; how rude not to give my name.
My Name is COCAINE!
ZS Argenio

Someone very dear to me is a recovering addict; the pain I saw in their eyes was so much it hurt me to see them like this. I tried everything I could, but nothing seemed to work as it needed to come from them. They needed to want to recover; they needed to be ready. I wrote them this poem to try and show in words what was happening to them, what they couldn't see. Once this person was willing, she put her all in, and she did it. As of writing this book, she has been clean for sixteen months. A journey that she decided to go on, healing and learning to love herself again, she is still on this journey, and she is doing so well. I couldn't be prouder of the person she is today. I want her to know how much we all love her and how we are so proud of the young lady she is today.

'Suicide'

Nothing so golden as my five-inch blade
In my depressed mind, I glorify it with a grade
This blade has become my absolute obsession
'Tis now like the ultimate profession
Caused by my sadness and depression!
I may overthink and procrastinate
Deep inside, I fear this now is my fate
I can feel myself giving in to these hell-hole voices
I've tried to drown them with loud noises
Only this doesn't work!
My head is telling me to do it
I try to fight it; I try all the time
Will I cut right through my vein?
I guess adrenaline will kick in, so there will be no pain
In my blood, I will fall and suffocate
With no one here to resuscitate!
This is my head, with the feeling of suicidal thoughts
I'm feeling sick now. My tummy is in knots
I know in reality that I have a disorder
Borderline Personality Disorder
To me, it feels like a living hell. My mind, I torture!
Please, please, someone help me with my breakdown
This is not a silly phase, nor one of meltdown

MENTAL HEALTH

It's serious, really, really serious
Certainly not something I want to experience
So, I'm begging for help to rid of this feeling
I ask you to start believing
Please don't leave me alone with depression and anxiety
Help me go back out to society
Help me, please
rid my mind of this disturbing disease
I don't want suicide
I desire a healthy mind
I don't want suicide
I don't want suicide!
ZS Argenio

'The Power of Love,'

Loving a child, nurturing, and worrying are the hardest things to do
Sometimes, you look for a window to see through
To the point of no return...
Something turns your insides upside down, and your belly churns!
Where's the way? You ask
As with everything you do, you try hard to grasp!
Hold on tight with every thought and peaceful power you have inside
No dignity you care; you swallow your pride
You hear the cries, the teardrops falling
You pray and hope he hears your calling
Help my child, free her from pain
Nothing inside is for you to gain
Only beauty to see, not hurt or pain
A smile, all laughter, every inch, you scream.....

Dear father, please, pull her out of this dream
Help her through it; give her your strength and love
From your lightened end and peaceful above!
Watch over her every second of every day
Please help me help her find her way

MENTAL HEALTH

No urges taking, just peace to find
Be a dad, seek inside her mind
For I know you hear my powerful cries
Of fear and worry, and I don't know how many 'whys'
Don't turn your head, don't you look away
Listen to me when to you, her father, I pray
Her sweet smile so pretty to see
Please help brighten it and keep it be
No place for return, for the earth is home
Beauty and integrity are never alone
Just be happy from now and heal in time
Please hear me and see through this rhyme
Let peace and harmony grab her tight
 Please help her fill herself with power and fight
Help end this chapter and begin a new
Life of love, kindness and courage, a smile through and through
Shining so bright, happy ending
Let your child's heart start mending!
Thank you for hearing and clearing the pain
Please keep it away, and never let this pain come back again

ZS Argenio
Written for one of my beautiful daughters.

Trying.'

Trying to get out of bed, it's hard
I'm sorry you were dealt this mental health card
Don't want to get dressed
Everything makes you scream and stressed
You force yourself to take a shower
That's even if you make it. Already you have cowered.
Drink your tea; at least try
But everything is an effort; you cry
Your PJs are stale from weeks of wearing
The four walls you carry on staring
Nothing can shift the darkness
As you seep into depression, you regress
Thoughts that battle you every day
No matter how hard you try, they won't go away
Scars, the power from your blade
Let me take it, don't be afraid
Ashamed inside
So instead, you will hide
Your senses go hell into overdrive
From fighting back trauma, you survived
You're worried about talking to someone
Worried about being judged, this is how far it's come
I'm here to tell you; it's ok not to be ok

MENTAL HEALTH

My heart will listen to all you have to say
I'm here to hold your hand
For as long as it takes, we will make a stand
Fight it together, so you're not alone.
I will help you pick up that phone
I will stand by you
I will be here for you
You don't have to suffer in silence
I will be here as your guidance
Hold on, my friend,
As of now, you no longer have to pretend
You are not the burden you believe yourself to be
So please, let me help you; your mind becomes free.

ZS Argenio

'They Say.'

They say that the reason is stress
Why your mind is in such a mess
They tell you don't listen to the voice
Allow yourself to prey and rejoice
Only it doesn't always work
Something else more powerful takes over
You face it; you know it's coming closer
Your fear is deep, with nowhere to go
Each story's narrative is all you know
You ask yourself a million times:
You look for answers in your rhymes
Only what you seek, you can't find
It's all stuck inside your mind
So, all you have is hope and prayer
Is it enough, in the mirror, you stare
You see it all; each word has an image
each image has its ending, its finish
What are you supposed to do with that
You leave it untouched, just like that
For now, they say, enough is enough!
ZS Argenio

'A Web'

I can't get it in my head; I don't seem to understand
It's like you always have the upper hand
You take a stand
At that moment, you mean all you say
You don't play with your words; you give them hard
In my hand, a card
I have to read it and play ball
In my head, to my knees, I fall
Each sentence with my body, I crawl
Within an inch again, I'm scared I will fall
The moment of speech
Sticks to me like a leach
Sucks my blood
Drains me; my brain has flood
I can't take hold,
Nor be bold,
As these words in my head unfold
These are all from my actions, I'm told
I worry about losing sight
I'm holding on with my bare hands so tight
My head the wounds, I put up this fight
The words linger
Becoming nearer

I fear the end
I worry for myself, the bits of me that no one can see
A dangerous enemy
If it is to be set free
My thoughts are my enemy
Each night in my head
I fight these demons instead of sleep
For there I lay, inside it creeps
Like a spider on a web
A fly caught as it said

"I will wrap you with silk; slowly, you will drown with my web all around; you can't move, for, in this, you're stuck! Not much air, for now, nothing will compare your feelings of escape. Your mind belongs to me. Not now will you see, not now will you fight, around you I will squeeze tight.
ZS Argenio.

MENTAL HEALTH

'I wish.'

I wish I could see the world in a better way
I wish I knew all the right things to say
I wish I knew how to keep my mind at bay
I wish I knew how to make the thoughts go away
I wish I knew how to have a smile to stay
I wish I could turn my head to the sadness and say, 'no way'
I wish I was always cheerful and did not feel so grey
I wish I could hold my head high; only on my pillow do I lay
I wish people would understand me, never leave or go away
I wish my head would not be astray
I wish my emotions would learn it's ok not to be ok
I wish that God would hear me when I prey
I wish I could move this pain
From within me again
I wish it away
But what can I say
There seems to be no way
I don't want it here to stay
Please, God, take this pain away.
ZS Argenio

'Living'.

I live a life of loneliness and emptiness
All of which become less and less
I don't understand why I feel this pain
Maybe it's the fact that what I lose, never will I gain
To be able to live life to the full
Becomes un-lively and willing to pull
Understanding my thoughts of love and hope
Always ends up so that I can't cope
But why is this happening? Please tell me so
The unknown fact is that I don't know
But for me, the future, the truth is to be
That me myself will indeed be free!
From Me (Written in 1993)

'Dead Head Of Mine'

My mind disappeared with the hectic start
Of the day ahead, we would soon part
You would go your way
A new me for today
You told me that if I looked, I would see
But anxiety took over me.
You told me not to worry
That there was indeed no hurry
I allowed your voice to guide me through
I listened while you told me what to do
Assurance that it would be ok
That in good; this was the way
Only for me, it was not
Everything you said, I had forgot
It has all gone, just like that
And I'm still here, stuck in my flat
I'm never going to be able to go
To leave my mind, as you said so.
You lied to me; I believed you
You promised to help me through
Lie Lie Lie
Please leave me alone, goodbye!
ZS Argenio

'Unspoken'

So much pain
It hurts; my head hurts
I'm a burden
I don't want to be a burden, much sadness behind the eyes
Cries can be heard from the inside
The mind, silent to others
No one can find
Any hurt in me
For blind
They cannot see
I try to inform in ways that cannot speak
Troubles are worn, and my body is weak
Staring into the distance
Without listening
To my unspoken word
For its not heard
A mountain of problems
Reaches the surface
Always untold
Heart turns cold
Distance grows strong
Minds happy thoughts are gone

MENTAL HEALTH

They fade so far
In the future unclear
That seems so near
It feels so clear
No love can hold on
For again gone
Mind to shame
The heart in pain
Sorrow takes over, often
yet forgotten
ZS Argenio

CHAPTER 2

Love

Spoken word is poetry read out aloud. When one reads a poem out loud, it reads with integrity. It has so much emotion that the sound echoes into the mind, and you create your piece of beautiful scenery, and with each word and each sentence, a picture in your mind forms, creating a love story. It could be the birds flying above you blending into your mind, the sound the birds make. It could be the trees whistling behind you that then becomes a framework of two loved ones holding hands, walking in the forest with the wind softly hitting the trees giving the sound of the leaves rustling as you walk. The birds singing and chirping away sets the romance scene; of course, all this is in one's imagination from the sounds you hear.

In the chapter, I have included a poem I wrote from a wife to her husband. When I was asked to do it, I didn't hesitate, the wife was leaving for another country on holiday for a few weeks, and her husband was to stay behind; the separation was a lot for them both; I was approached and asked how to put words together to form a unique piece of love. I was left to my own devices, did so and titled the poem 'My Love.'

I'm so blessed to be able to write for others just as I do for myself.

'The Rose,'

A rose that sheds its petals
Is one that sheds its tears
We don't know why this happens
can only be through its fears
The rose was picked from a family tree
Yet the rest was left behind
'But why me?' This rose asks
You see, this rose was very kind
With the rose's heart so pure
yet its soul is so broken
It was specially picked with a golden token
To be given its place
To find its way
the rose needed the guidance of the hands; it would stay
So now you have this rose safe and warm
The seas it's battled not to be torn
Please hold it close with all your heart
As today you tell, this is the start
So all the fears the pure rose weeps
Will now turn into your greatest keeps.
I love you
ZS Argenio
Written for my dearest Anna.

'My Love,'

Memories to keep a beautiful picture book
Open this with me; let's take a look

Delightful feelings, intense lust
Down the marital aisle was a must
Our love, so often captured
Never expire; always a new chapter
Beautiful moments, so very divine
Although apart, our stars align
Hands gently cupped, the morning hour
Vulnerability, you always empower
Blinded by pleasure, so strong
Our beating hearts is not wrong
One motive, pure love and attraction
Between us, only true passion
Your tender touch, inner destiny
Cheek to cheek, pure ecstasy
Eyes in love, our heart's true desire
Bodies entwined, souls on fire
A moment of silence, so captivating
Pleasure belongs to you; I am waiting
ZS Argenio
Written for Braxton from his love, Andrea.

"I WANT TO LET YOU INTO A SECRET, SHHH, YOU ARE MY SECRET."

ZS Argenio

'My Star,'

The night is dark
The stars glitter bright
Which one are you?
I ask as I turn out the light

I sit back in my chair
And wait for the brightest star
Now I can see you
You're not even that far

I miss you when the day comes
For the light dims your smile
But here you are, shining bright
Let me watch you for a while
ZS Argenio

"I KNOW WE ARE SOUL MATES BECAUSE EVERY TIME I HEAR YOUR HEART BEATING, I CAN FEEL MINE BEAT AT THE SAME TIME."

ZS Argenio

'Missed You,'

Where did you go?
What did you see?
How did you get there?
Did you miss me?

I worried for a while
That you weren't coming back
Reassurance was what we needed
Now we are back on track
ZS Argenio

> "I KNOW WHEN YOU ARE AROUND BECAUSE MY HEART FILLS WITH BUTTERFLIES."

ZS Argenio

'The Eve Night,'

I waited for the door to open
A key was needed
A key to a door
The door to my heart
It came on the eve night
When time stood still
But eyes wide open
The Key was found
And indoor was open
Pain poured out
On lonely night, skies
The stars are always distant
Alone for out of sight
Now belonging to the opener of heart
For she shall fill the wound
With laughter and happiness
Tears of joy stood still
And one heart became two
Conjoined, a pack was made
that only love would fill two hearts
As time went on
The hearts bound more together
The love encircled

LOVE

Entwined in souls
Only happiness thrives
With two love's power
By each side
Time grows old
As did two hearts
Found was once
For now eternity
A promise of love
Two hearts now, one
Never to be broken
The pair set sail
Their journey
That very eve night

ZS Argenio
Written for my dear love Anna.

> **"I DO NOT NEED A REASON TO LOVE YOU; I LOVE YOU."**
>
> ZS Argenio

'Our Forever,'

I remember the first time our eyes met
The beauty of two souls, we will never forget
Our hearts became so shy, but the want was very clear
To hold each other so close, so near
In my eyes, you looked deeper
I knew then you would become my keeper
You pulled me so close to you
That's when I knew
Our love would be true.
You placed your lips on mine and kissed me softly
I didn't want you to stop; I didn't want you off me
Everything around us fell so silent
It felt as though we were on a beautiful island
Alone, just the two of us together
That's when we started our forever
ZS Argenio
Written for my dear Anna

'I Spy,'

If I could spy
Something in my eye
I wonder what it would be.

An Image of you
An image of me
That's what I would see
ZS Argenio

> "KISS ME GOOD MORNING, KISS ME GOODNIGHT, AND NEVER FORGET I LOVE YOU."
>
> ZS Argenio

'Your Touch,'

Soft kiss sets the eve
Known, not one will leave
Love between us just begun
As entwined, our bodies become
I lay across you bare
Our passion fills the air
Beneath the sheets, we shiver
Tangled in ore, we quiver
A deep touch felt
Within you, I melt
Our hands astray
Filled with ecstasy, we may
Our souls on fire
flames of desire
As our souls become one
Till the morning sun

ZS Argenio

'What'

What does one expect?
When nothing is expected
What does one do?
When one is rejected.

What does one try?
When it's all out, trying
What does one do?
When one is always crying.

What does one mean?
When there's no more meaning
What does one do?
When inside, one is screaming.

What does one say?
When all is wrong in saying
What does one do?
When what's left is preying.

The answer lies with truths untold
So, one must now be honest
What does one do, then?
Go with her and make that promise.
ZS Argenio.

'Love And Lust'

Entwined we meet
Eyes they greet
Passion is near
Body in fear
Of love and lust
Indeed, a must
To close together
Comforted forever
In the arms of your love
Like a flying dove
Erotic pours the night
Body in all its might
Of love and lust
Together now a must
No delicate touch
Is too much
Goosebumps belong
With you not wrong
Love in each other
For not another

My one

My first love has begun.

ZS Argenio

Written for you, my dear Anna.

CHAPTER 3

World

(TRIGGER WARNING THROUGHOUT THIS CHAPTER)

Everybody sees the world in their way; I want to tell you how I see it.

One thing I know is that the world is such a beautiful place. (God) Mother nature created a beautiful planet to share, live on, and have our existence. We share our world with many different species, some that we don't even know about. From mammals to animals, insects to fish and plants, nature and humans. Forgive me if I left anything out.

One thing I don't understand is war. Humans have been battling one another since the beginning of time and still do in the present. Why fight when we can have love? Why do humans do their utmost to destroy the very thing we call home? If I could make one wish, it would be to stop all the wars and have peace.

To me, what's important in my heart is 'Love' and 'Peace' I can't stand cruelty to one another, people who are racist and prejudiced against their fellow human beings; this I will never understand.

Children are not born racist; sadly, in our world, we are all products of our environment; unless people are willing to educate themselves and learn to be better versions of themselves, there will always be cruelty in this world.

Our planet is unique; it provides food, water, friendships and love. (not all of us can see that)

When writing this book, the world was in a state of emergency due to the pandemic Covid 19; since finishing the book, part of Europe has gone to war. (as well as all the other wars and hatred going on around the globe.)

The first poem of the chapter is in memory of all black lives lost or still suffering at the hands of the racist!

'Black Lives Matter'

As I stood there and photographed the beautiful strawberry moon
I thought to myself, my soul, a question: how can we unite and be in tune?
With this, I mean beauty in all human life
With love all to give, like I and my wife
We need the power of knowledge to educate all human beings
Learn about 'white privilege,' listening to everyone's feelings
As a white woman, I have 'white privilege'
Like all white folk in cities, towns and villages
Do I understand it?
Do you understand it?
We must understand what it means in every single aspect
Going back through history, White men, with all respect
While black people are mistreated, inhuman and unkind
It doesn't bear to think about in my mind
Only it is real, as real as your eyes reading this book
So please, I urge you, change is present; back at history, you must look

I state and will state that no life matters until Black Lives Matter
Don't just be and listen to the chatter
Do something, be that change
Don't be part of the oppression. Don't be deranged
Educate now and be part of the present change
We should have learnt by now that a change should have happened long ago,
Except.....
We ignored. Black Lives torn apart, belittled, like some sick show!
Black mothers protecting their young from the sours of White
Black men were gunned down for protecting their families and putting up a fight!
I ask you to educate, please, just as the sun sets and the moon arises
I pray to myself that the new dawn will bring positive surprises
Of peace, tranquillity, and love
Understanding ourselves and teaching our young
So, in the future, no cruelty; as we give education, positivity will come
To bring about speech and say to all human race that we are one

Never be afraid to speak out, do so in love and honour,
Help white people educate; let's stop this cycle, unite, and become stronger.
To unite means to learn and understand Black Lives culture
And stop the white man acting like we are all dividing vultures!
We must learn with our hearts, with our heads and stop to think
What have we learnt? Allowing history to repeat, we can be that missing link
Educate, educate, educate 'White privilege'
We all can have hearts of forgiveness
So let us all remind ourselves to make a change, remind ourselves to remember,
we are not cruel, racist members
only pure of love and great defenders
of Black Lives
So, like the sunsets and the moon arises,
we will be ready to unite with inspiring surprises
with this, we will know no one matters until Black Lives Matter!
We can change the path of the present and future,
Let's get rid of all the cruel, horrid, racist torture.

I will begin and pray for change, peace and love, honour and respect
every one of all 'White Privilege', please learn, educate and always protect
In memory of all Black Lives lost from the torture of racism.
ZS Argenio

"BE YOUR OWN EXPECTATIONS, SO MAKE THEM COUNT."

ZS Argenio

'Covid-19'

As I laugh and play out in the sun
I know in my mind it is all just fun
Then out of nowhere, a virus sweeps through towns and cities
We would learn to rise above, come together and give no pity
This thing, it landed with a crash, suddenly it's here
We had no time to prepare, so we sat in fear!
The virus carried on ripping through towns and cities
We joined united and gave it no pity
What do we do?
For this all together, we must get through
Let us use old-fashioned imagination
For now, the world is in lockdown
We need to use our brain's creation
We taught our young to cook
We inspired the elderly with meditation and reading a good old book!
People shared their thoughts across the internet
Showing the bravery of Drs and Nurses in helping the sick
Most definitely something the world will never forget
On our doors at six pm every night

WORLD

We shared our gratitude to the NHS as we all unite
As this virus sweeps through towns and cities
Together we learnt to give the virus no pity
So many people were stuck solely inside
For fear, they had heard that one more person had died
A world filled with sadness, teardrops from eyes to lip
We raise a glass in memory; we take a sip
I urge you, people, to come out to play
Remember your smile and the words you say
I'm laughing now, and I'm out in the sun.
The new normal, I'm just having fun.
ZS Argenio

'War,'

I used to think this world was beautiful
Everything about it, from summer to autumn fall
I couldn't wait to wake up in the morning and feel the day ahead
Now I wake with one feeling of only dread
With the war in Ukraine
Everyone around the world is feeling the strain
Unprecedented attacks on towns and cities
To you, Mr P, we give no pity
Your sharp exits to a bunker of gold, no doubt
While your people are out there to you, they shout....
Dear Mr P
Please ask your soldiers to put down their guns,
So mothers can again hold their sons
please don't let them die for no real reason
Don't allow history to know you as the man of murder and treason
Pull out your soldiers, call off this war
Help build up Ukraine as it was before
Do something good. We know you can.
Help the matter that is now on your hands
For future history will be saddened by what you did
When children learn at school what Mr P did

WORLD

When they hear the broken hearts of a story told
By your people, the ones you pledged and promised to hold!
Future will learn of the people of Ukraine and the courage that was to unfold
From Ukrainian people during a war, yet their hearts were of gold
Their President is out there (in the midst of a war) with his people
As well as still keeping everything legitimate and legal
While you, Mr P, the future children, will learn of murder and torture!
For what, a power of bad will and that of miss fortune?
Please stop, we beg you, as the president of your country
Let history see that you stopped this and allowed people to be free
Your people will forgive you for the good of their hearts
As your people didn't want any war to start.
Now lay down your weapons; the world begs Mr P
to stop your soldiers from unnecessarily shooting.
Help the Ukrainians shake hands with President Z
Help unite, please, and let everyone be free!
ZS Argenio

"LIVE THE LIFE YOU WANT, NOT THE LIFE SOMEONE ELSE WANTS YOU TO LIVE. DO SO WITH LOVE."

ZS Argenio

'Listen,'

All the negative paths we're consuming
Like caged animals, except we are human
This is no longer funny or amusing
Not everything we do is a bad mistake
But your human era is what's a disgrace!
We work hard to become a society that's restored
Only yet again, you want to involve us in war
Enough lives have already been sacrificed
Yet still, you're far from satisfied
So, on behalf of the people, I speak..
Don't make us an enemy for the glory you seek
Instead, use your power to free us from anxiety
Do not burden us, instead make us your priority
Not again; let us seep these wounds that don't heal
Just because you made a promise, in turn, a good deal
We beg you, don't use weapons of mass destruction
Instead, listen to us and rid your corruption
Please don't allow us to be once again divided
Rather, please keep us all united
Give us the reason we need to hold your trust

With all your people, we believe you will and can adjust
No more wars, no frightened families
Do the one thing that should come naturally
Peace and love, let us live in harmony
ZS Argenio

'Our World'.

Our world is coming to a poor end
So no longer can we pretend
Some of it is down to us because we pollute the air
But then, sometimes life isn't fair.

It's not just that; its animals and nature too
For those people, they shoot the animals just for something to do.
But they never think that it brings tears and sadness
Because our wildlife is becoming less and less.

They shoot the birds down from the sky
And then sit back and watch them die
They never think for a moment how these birds must feel
Otherwise, they wouldn't do such a thing; it can't be real!

One day these people are going to sit there in terra
And know they have made one big era
So, something must be done
For this fantasy is no longer fun!
From me (Written in 1993)

'The Flower Too The Bee'

As it rains, flowers glorify
Not letting a drop pass by
A source of food they give
Provide for bees to help them live.
So, flowers begin to spring open
All the bees they are hoping
Will come and visit the flower
In bloom, they wait the passing hour
A beauty of scents descends in the air
Open petals and pollen to share
One bee, two bees, now there are three
Collecting pollen for their master honey-bee
As they buzz and fly away
They thank 'flower' for their wonderful stay
Flowers must now close their petals
For night, under the stars, they nestle
They wimp silent until a new sunrise
Where again flower, for bees, will come alive.
ZS Argenio.

'Creating'

Creating is a journey of its own
The eyes that's on the project know
One tiny little mistake
Must be corrected, not given to take
Hard work and honour from the heart
Goes into every detail from the start
From materials to pick
And colours you know will stick
To make the project come to life
We use our best carving knife
Following our instruction
Creating our new invention
God gave us the ability
To be full of creativity
To bring happy faces all around
With a gift from our minds, we found.
By ZS Argenio

'A Temper From Sour Takes'

So divine is the world we have
One earth for all existence
One flower to wilt for thee
A temper from sour takes
Soil in hold of warmth
To feed the inner strength
A temper from sour takes
Tree grows tall
Home to creatures
A temper the sour takes
A wall built to heal
yet fallen in greed
A temper the sour takes
Sea will battle
droplets to steal
A temper the sour takes
leave alone
let freedom grow
No temper a sour to take.
By ZS Argenio
For Mother Nature!

"WE ARE ALL INDIVIDUALS; WE ARE ALL UNIQUE. ONE THING WE HAVE IN COMMON IS THAT WE ARE ALL FROM PLANET EARTH. WE ALL HAVE A HEART THAT BEATS FOR US TO LIVE, SO PLEASE LIVE WITH LOVE IN YOUR HEART FOR EVERYONE. STOP THE CRUELTY, PAIN AND SUFFERING. YOU CAN STILL CHANGE; YOU STILL HAVE THE ABILITY TO CHANGE FOR THE BETTER."

ZS Argenio

CHAPTER 4

Self Image

(TRIGGER WARNING THROUGHOUT THIS CHAPTER)

Courage is a small word with an enormous meaning, and the intention is all yours to decide what you want from it. I challenge myself every day to have the courage to do something different. For me, courage is a big part of my everyday life. It's a part of who I am. Courage, along with other words, manifests itself in our daily life, like self-esteem, love, belonging, self-worth, and so many more. They are all essential to help with our well-being. How do you work with your courage? What gives you the courage to have courage? Meditation helps me allow myself to look in the mirror and love what I see back. So many of us in today's society want to be someone else. We get so fixated on social media in someone else's life that we forget our own. We stop feeling beautiful. How many times a day do you browse through your phone, looking at other people wishing you either had what they had, or you looked just like they do? How often do you punish yourself for not being good enough because of what you have seen on your phone? What were our lives like before social media took its place on the stage, before we spent hours a day staring into a black hole, getting sucked into rabbit holes, and turning our belief systems upside down? Who were we? What would happen if it was all taken away from us? Filters on snapshots we take of ourselves can be so harmful.

We forget our true beauty and rely on what the app on the internet is offering us. We are very impressionable when we are younger. Some of us are still in our later years, with low self-esteem and no courage to feel confident. We continue to put each other down through the use of the internet. What do all the filters teach the younger generation about them? It certainly doesn't desire their beauty but that of someone else; they stop seeing themself and pledge their looks to what is no longer reality.

Many people across all age groups, genders and sexualities find it hard to fit in. Many of our younger generations find themself at the mercy of others through peer pressure, especially online and with this can come much trouble for our youngsters. How do we resolve such a complex society when most counties don't have enough funds to help eliminate the risks that can occur across our internet platforms?

If there were more groups and youth clubs for our younger generation and support for parents and caregivers, it would eliminate much stress and worry; this could be done by educating adults about internet use with youngsters. The children would have somewhere to explore a wide range of things about themself, including their feelings.

The feeling of power can elect such control in oneself, which gets one into trouble. Therefore, we must help teach our children about self-respect and respecting others. We need to help them grow with healthy confidence and incredible self-esteem. Our children will, of course, make mistakes, and they will learn to take accountability for their actions. If you instil these tremendous and essential life skills from a young age, especially about loving themselves, it will help them in their future; I'm not going to say that once you have executed this, you will have perfect children because there is no such thing as 'perfect'. Still, it will help them to understand themselves, especially when puberty hits. Moody teenagers and peer pressure is a crucial time for our youngsters; our duty as adults, parents and caregivers is to listen to them and learn to read their body language. We want our children to feel beautiful and understand that sometimes it's ok not to feel ok; they are learning too. Teaching a child about consequences comes with an excellent ability to understand that you can't always do what you want to do.

Children and adults want to fit in, and sometimes the desperation goes too far! Because what you see in your mirror is not the reflection you want to see; you want to look like the person you saw on the internet. Cameras and phones allow you to change how you look, how our children look, and how society looks; it's called a filter! More significant fuller lips, more lifted eyebrows, higher cheekbones and a jawline that is so sharp it puts a ruler to shame! This is real life, and it is happening all around us. This is happening to our children and parents/caregivers, who no longer want to grow old peacefully and gracefully; that time has gone. What if someone's mother was to go missing, and the only pictures you had of your mother were a real-time photo of her in her twenties or a fake face-lifting filter that swarms her entire social media? This is where we all are? Most of us, anyway? How many of you reading this book, this chapter, can say you have used a filter and felt so much better about yourself for it? How many of your children or siblings have a complete set of fake photos on social media?

It is a bit like the new 'Cat Fishing. You go on a dating site to meet Mr/Miss, right? The first thing we are all guilty of is looking at the photograph of the person/persons. We look, then we may read the profile and say a conversation starts, and the next thing you know, you have agreed to meet in a beautiful place (a place of safety always, please). You get dressed in your best outfit, with your matching colour shoes to your handbag (assuming you're a woman), your hair all curled, and you have on your fake eyelashes; your makeup is not over the top but classy, and boom, you look beautiful. You head down to your car, that excitement hits your tummy, butterflies fill, and nerves go ten to the dozen; you reach your destination and park up. There you are, just standing, looking toward your designated meet place, let's say Costa Coffee, that's a safe place, you're waiting for her (assuming in this one it's a woman), she still hasn't arrived, you have walked over now and taken a seat, you're all alone you decide to take your order of expresso and wait!

How long are you waiting for, because just opposite your table is another woman who is also alone, looking around, waiting to meet someone? That someone is you. She does not know you have arrived because you look nothing like your photo, your lips aren't plumped like the actress you admire, your hair is not long blonde with low lights, and you're not a size zero; in fact, you are a beautiful healthy size 14, with lovely long locks, a thin top lip with the bluest of eyes, you are gorgeous, you just forgot, so of course, this person doesn't know you have arrived because you look nothing like your photo. The same as the woman you are waiting for; it is, in fact, the lady who made herself look so youthful for her age. She filtered out all the fine lines on her face; she made her hair a light brown, slightly lifted her eyebrows so the stripes on her forehead would disappear, and gave herself a younger appearance when in reality, the person you are meeting has aged well, she has all those fine lines, her hair is going grey, she has smoker lines from when she used to smoke, but she also forgot that she was beautiful. So now what? You both go home and think they stood you up? Or do you send a text revealing your nerves, but you have arrived, and you're seated?

Let's go with the text scenario. OK, you have sent the message, you wait for your response, and you get it, 'hey beautiful, where are you? I can't see you; I'm sitting on the table to the left of the door. Find me and come over. I'm nervous too, but I can't wait to meet you.' You now know the person sitting in front of you is your online date! Now I'm hoping in my imagination that with all the beautiful messages you have been sending each other and how you have been building each other's confidence up, you won't be shallow; you will see past each other's looks, sit down to coffee, get on like a house on fire, realise the beauty in each other is better in real life than that of a filter and live happily ever after, but that unfortunately is not reality.

You have all, I'm sure, been there; your body is too fat or too thin, you have noticed more fine lines coming, your skin is not soft enough, you have a spot on your face, and to you, it is the end of the world. We all understand and can relate to this feeling of not being good enough, whether with our image or our everyday life trying to be. We should all empower and help each other feel beautiful and valued. If we spread love and fulfilment over social media without a filter, just be us, be the real you, show who you are, and don't be afraid. Look in that mirror and tell yourself every day that 'you are good enough' get undressed every day, no clothes, just your skin and look at yourself from the top of your head to your toes in the mirror and practise the words 'I am beautiful' start instilling this is your mind, it will take time, but it will happen. Then their environment will change when your children see you smiling like really smiling, full of healthy confidence and feeling beautiful. They will see themself just as beautiful if we could change social media by first starting the change in ourselves.

The poetry you will read below is about social media, filters and self-image. I got poorly with a disease called Multiple Sclerosis; this was such a life-changing event for my family and me; I found myself in a deep hole, having to learn to use all my motor skills. I was very blessed to have the help and support of my children; believe me when I say I didn't make this easy for them; my reason was that I had always suffered from self-image problems and body dysmorphia, so to now have something that was debilitating was so hard I did stop loving myself. I, too, took to social media and filtered every image I sent or added to make myself look better. I struggled increasingly with poor eating and gaining weight due to medication. I couldn't find it in me to have self-love. I didn't feel beautiful, and my self-esteem had

SELF IMAGE

hit the floor. Like many of the population today, I forgot that I was indeed beautiful, just like you are.

'Filter'

I need a selfie 'Snap'
oh no, I don't look good in that
my lips are most definitely too thin
I also need a white tooth grin
As well as a chiselled chin
Remove all my fine lines
Take my face back to more youthful times
I know, an eyebrow lift
I can make it ombre, oh what a gift
I may as well slim down my arms
They're too fat, so it won't do any harm
Now to change my hair
It's only fair
As long as it's not mine, I don't care
What colour will I choose?
A colour to match my shoes
Now to change my nose
Make it pointier, I suppose
I will also add a nose ring
change my eye colour too, that's a thing

SELF IMAGE

Wow

Look at me now

I don't even recognise myself

I wonder, will anyone else?

By ZS Argenio

"LOOK INTO THE MIRROR AND STARE INTO YOUR EYES; WHAT YOU ARE SEEING IS YOUR BEAUTY STARING RIGHT BACK AT YOU."

ZS Argenio

'Courage,'

I look at you, yes you, detangling your hair, at your face, you stare, giving yourself that disastrous glare.

This glare gives no self-affection, only a slum of digestion of what you see.
Again I look at you, wondering who the reflection is with no self-affection, like you're hoping for an election of what you see.

Looking at you tear yourself apart, giving yourself red dots on a chart, like you're beating from a broken heart. You know you have the power to heal this with your art!

Now I stare at you. I can only hear the cries, as inside, I know you want to say your goodbyes. I can see from this the pain it would have upon others if you did.

Come on, pick up, start a new; come back happy from blue; you may not yet even have a clue of what you're to do!
Only you've got this, as I know you

You think you can't undo what you think has failed. I see you;
I'm telling you nothing has failed, only ended. It's not like you pretended to make the extended version of a light that yearns to shine so bright all day till night.

Empty the feeling of panic, dissolve the misery, and surrender your negative feelings.
Start believing that achieving you to be happy, please, it's important.

Find the courage to be brave. You're not a slave to yourself.
The best of wealth is the happiest of health.

I'm looking at you still, with the will that you will feel how you truly want to.
I know I can find this somewhere inside of you.
A happy face, even if it's at the slowest pace, finding yourself is not a race.
It's in your hands and grace, you will find your happy place.

Remember, standing tall and looking fine is always your beauty in line.

SELF IMAGE

Try not to look behind, for not there will you find. Look in front, open your mind.
Have courage and be kind, for my dear, I, the reflection upon first eye detection.
I AM YOU.

I am the best version of you waiting to surface, for us as one for each other we serve a purpose.
I beg of you, don't be nervous, be certain that the beauty in you; is what you will now see.

Make up off your hair all down, loosen up, relax, and put on your beautiful crown, rid yourself of this negativity, hurt, and pain.
There is no shame in feeling and owning your beauty, as there is no blame in not!

Learn how to look in the mirror with a humble smile, and I, who is you, will look back at you with an even bigger smile.
For you are me, and I am your courage.
ZS Argenio

'You Will Make Me Fat'

I see you time and time again
In my head, I tell myself it's never the same
Yet as I wander through the pathways
In my brain, memory
All I ever see is you, my thoughts directory
It's hard to understand, as you had me right there
A once upon a time is now, beware
Would you answer if you could?
You make me fat!
Would you say significantly, so I understood
Remember, a flower sewn
Grown
Entwined
Sometimes intense, thus cannot unwind
Reveal the truth, powers of my once gold dust
Now I look at you in disgust
You make me fat!
Would you ever look and wish behind?
Struggle real, in the unconscious mind
For branches, all fell
When broke, I could never tell
Every tabletop and plated food
Ultimately in stone was my mood

SELF IMAGE

You make me fat!
A secret held to the happiest humbled
If ever told, minds would become crumbled
Nothing would ever be as it seemed
Unless out loud, I screamed
The tabletop was deemed
Nothing would be set in stone
forever stuck in the mind's unknown
Because you make me fat!
By ZS Argenio

'Mis - Fit'

Miss-Fire Miss-Haps Miss-Fits all in one
For when it happens, they will leave you with no fun
The unseen, unheard, forgotten thoughts, feelings suppressed
Like a mirror image of the mind naked, undressed
A reflection in front, on hold
Your mind on its own reflected but un-told
Harbour the power, the fight that's inside
For only you alone yourself to guide
Your memory is frozen, sunken, unshielded
Vulnerability unprotected, you knew this indeed
What do you do? What's the right thing to say?
Must be the truth, for the time will come, and they will pay
Miss-Fire, Miss-Haps Miss-Fits all in one
You come, remove my fun
Pride, figurines, love, honesty and protect
Keep yourself together; you must remember the 'subject'
Will this be now? Will this be the narrow path I walk?
For a mind flooded, no time to talk
Miss-Fire, Miss-Haps, Miss-Fits all in one
Again, you come to remove my innocent, fun

SELF IMAGE

I feel strange but strong, my brain all wired
So much to deal with, but in mind, never tired
Windows all darkened, a room with no shine
You took from me what was forever mine.
No mirror, no reflection will show me the truth, just pain
For it was your pleasure, your gain.
Nails all bitten and mind awake.
Of course, you're here again. Take, take, take!
Miss-Fire, Miss-Haps, Miss-Fits all in one
You're always there, removing my fun
No smile real
Red cheeks to steal
Confused and angered is all
You take my power, my solace, to that I fall
In the darkness, I'm frightened, do not pity me
Otherwise, come my tears and sadness. This can and must not be!
Allow me to go freeze, flight or fight
In distance afar, let there be something good in sight
For you know, and I know
Deep in my heart, I must let it go
For you can see me in mind, I always see you
Miss-Fire, Miss-Haps, Miss-Fits, this is what you do!
ZS Argenio

'TV'

These days I don't like to switch on my television
For fear of what's going on in the world
One minute its war
The next is arguments in politics
We have nurses going on strike
and rightly so
Up their pay
that's what I say.
ZS Argenio

'My Kingdom'

I felt it as it breezed past me
I could smell the bittersweet
I could sense the timing was right
For now, you were at my feet

I looked so bewildered
And wondered what I would say
So, a thought passed my lips
Out loud, I wasn't afraid

I felt steady and sure
That the time was right
So aloud I spoke
This wasn't a fight

I sought it as a whole
Nothing more behind
For the new me began
And I was not hard to find

Now you may leave
Don't surface your head again
For I am my kingdom
The negativity you will refrain!
ZS Argenio

SELF IMAGE

'Look In The Mirror'

They say in the mirror is your reflection
Stare back; it's not an objection
It is you, the real you
Open your eyes is what you must do
Look right into your own eyes
Try and blank out your silent cries
Of hate towards your skin
That you are too fat and not thin
A line here, a line there
To yourself, you are not being fair
Change your thought pattern
Come down from planet Saturn
Back to earth, take another look
Then write this in your book
Your eyes are big and bright
Your cheeks are lifted, and light
Your lips are pretty, delicate
You are not desolate
Your face tells your story
In all beauty and glory

Let yourself shine; you need to see
So, open your eyes and let the mind free
Smile to yourself; your reflection will smile back
Keep the happy face on track
Just by trying every single day
A look in the mirror your way
And tell yourself you are enough.
By ZS Argenio

SELF IMAGE

'Be Like You'

I wish I could look like that
I hope I can be like you
Except I'm nothing like that
And I'm nothing like you

I wish I could do what you do
I hope I could have all that you have
Except I can't do what you do
And I can't have what you have

Why do I want to be like you
Your just someone on my phone
Why can't I love me
My face, my skin and my bone

Instead, I stare at my reels.
Over and over again
And wish it was all me
But it's not, and it's not the same
ZS Argenio

'Image'

I put on my make-up
And do up my hair
I look in the mirror
And I do not care
I love what I see
And I wish you did too
For I am the mirror image
And you're beautiful through and through
ZS Argenio

SELF IMAGE

'Love Yourself'

A caring nature and a kind heart
Is all you need to have
So, stop being vain
And appreciate what you have

Don't look at your phone
If you have no self-control
Instead, remind yourself of beauty
And take back that control

If you don't love yourself
Then how can you love another
Tell yourself you're enough
Then you won't want to be another

Your beauty goes beyond your eyes
And straight into your heart
So, stop trying to be someone else
Because you have the best heart
ZS Argenio

> "LEARN TO BE IN TUNE WITH YOURSELF FIRST; THEN YOU WILL UNDERSTAND THE MUSIC OF OTHERS."
>
> ZS Argenio

CHAPTER 5

Nightmares

(TRIGGER WARNING THROUGHOUT THIS CHAPTER)

We all dream; some of us remember our dreams, and some do not. I am a person who remembers most of my dreams, a lot of which are, in fact, nightmares. I started having nightmares as a young child; these continued into my adulthood. I tried all sorts of meditations, ASMR and different sleep timings to help me with it. Nothing seemed to work, so I started a dream journal in which I wrote and expressed mine in poetry.

One dream I have is a false awakening; this can be so scary that I find myself walking around the house only to realise I'm still asleep, so I'm not walking around the house as I'm still sleeping. This can happen several times a night.

Another problem I have is my awake life, past and present, entering my dream space; some of these dreams again are nightmares. From what I understand, our brain stores hundreds and thousands, if not millions, of files, so everything we see in our dreams we have seen in real life. Our mind has a funny and sometimes scary way of putting things together and forming dreams, good or bad.

I am not a sleep Dr or a dream specialist; I only know what happens in my sleep with my dreams.

One thing I will say is that past trauma does play a significant part in my sleep life, which is one of the reasons I started journaling. Writing has always been a therapy; even though my trauma can come out in my sleep time, I try to remain positive upon waking.

I have a ritual I try to do every day when I wake up. I speak five things I appreciate in my life, I say them out loud, and I find it starts my day on a positive, whether I have slept well or poorly.

'Devil'

I know where you came from. I know the start
There is always a beginning, as well as an end to every part
Why do you feel as though nothing else matters?
Whatever has surfaced must indeed have a purpose
Is this making your insides crumble?
Making you feel as if you will fall and tumble?
This can never go in reverse
Within, right now, is all nerves
Head turned again into a circus
A horrid feeling like caged animals unknown in their path
Their nameless future, for unfed
Starved until dead!
Sad, unfair
This I will never prepare
Only wait it out, for I pray with each punch that strikes
You get lighter and lighter, you sin, the more you like!
Why can't you look for another way
Like a caged animal, you had me stay
Why can't I run?
I must run
Otherwise

You will see the fear in my eyes
You will look upon this as weakness and cries
The devil is in you, for to him you bound
Not a still drop of water, not a single sound
I can't make you leave this dream
For in you the devil shouts, the door will open,
For there, I will scream
Try to awaken from you the devil's dream
Instead, there I lay
The thought of the devil and what he did most every day
Has sent me into a frenzy
Realising I'm still asleep
I know you are there
In you, the devil's creep
I must hold on to reality
It's just a dream
For I'm no longer in this sick fuck's fantasy
My escape was a long time ago.
I need to wake up so I can see
So that you, the devil, will know
I will never be in the devil's existence
Remind me I'm strong and persistent
Listening to my awakened mind and knowing I can be resistant

NIGHTMARES

In time, I will keep this devil dream distant
Awaken my mind out of this dream
When the devil calls again upon my sleep
The retched voice, in mind it seeps
I remind myself that I'm in control
Living through hell is now in my unconscious mind
Remind me of this; that trapped feeling
So far away from my mind's mentality
I must try harder to free all brutality
Hopelessness and shame
Asleep again
'WAKE UP'
It's my mind's game
If I allow this devil to continue to enter my dream space
All I will have is this subconscious race
Then my awakened life will be full of fear and anxiety
Then gone will be my sobriety
It is not what I want
I will face it
 Fight it
Lift the burden of always being in, freeze, flight or fight all the time
Let the past stay in the past, then in time
Dreamtime will be fine!
I mustn't allow the devil to haunt my dreams

I refuse to give him my sadness and pain
Now I will try harder to refrain.
I have got this; lay myself down,
With the sound of the ocean,
I will feel the slow movement of an imaginative breeze
Let my body go with this motion.
Asleep, I will fall, the beauty of a pleasant dream will
begin, and I will not let you in this
time, you, the devil!
ZS Argenio

'The Gate'

Staying up late
Looking at the end of my gate
A strange man I see
Run I say
Run fast and free

As I write my poem,
Not knowing
What's coming my way
do I stay
While they pay
Or run and hide
Looking behind
From what I might find
Only what I see
Is a mirror image of me
Where is my appointee?
I need an escape
But no guarantee
Of freedom.

Staying up late
Looking at the end of my gate
A strange man, I see
Run I say
Run fast and free.

Freedom is what I seek
As I become weak
Feeling like an antique
As I try to tweak
The pale colour of my cheeks
For in the mirror, I critique my look
You are disgusted at how I look
Why?
I'm just someone you traded and took!
I scream
To the extreme
Wake up!

Staying up late
Looking at the end of my gate,
A strange man, I see.
Run I say
Run fast and free

NIGHTMARES

As I wake
I take
The ache
Of my heartbreak
As I shake, feeling cold
Hands I hold
In my head, I'm told
Take off the blindfold
For here, you're controlled
By you
So let go
For he that haunts my dream
As it seems
Is gone
As for myself, I say
Try to move on

No more staying up late
For there is no man at the gate
Just a string
Of bad dreams
The past is gone
The present I belong.
ZS Argenio

'I Dreamed a Dream, And You Was There'

I dreamed a dream, and you were there
I started to feel very scared
I looked around and saw only darkness
The light became less and less
You walked closer to me
Calm. I tried to be
You reached out a hand
I couldn't understand
For I dreamed this dream, and you were there
Wake up, wake up
Don't be scared.
ZS Argenio

'Run'

I looked at the bright blue sky
The clouds passing by
The leaves whistle aloud
A beautiful sight till I turned around
Run, run, I say run
Only my legs won't move at all
I'm stuck in slow motion; your name I call
Run, run, try harder
My legs won't work, the sky is darker
My heart is beating through my chest
My legs must work; I must not rest
Run; I can do it
I try to lift a leg bit by bit
It's not working; I'm stuck
Your name is closer
You cannot come over
Run, dam it, move
My body I disapprove
If it does not work, I am stuck
Wake up, Wake up, Wake up.
ZS Argenio

'Asleep or?'

My eyes are closed, and I am drifting off
To a land of merry dreams, I hope
Except not this time
I'm scared, and I cannot cope

I realise I am asleep
Or am I actually awake
for this thing sits on my chest
The weight I cannot take

I try to move only I am paralysed
I try to scream, but nothing comes out
This thing has me
I need to scream and shout

Wait, my eyes are open
I can see I am awake
I get up and move around
Wait, I've made a mistake

NIGHTMARES

I'm still lying right here
I didn't wake up
The thing still crushing me
I can't breathe; set me free.
ZS Argenio

'Am I Awake?'

I am making a noise
But no one can hear me
I've been asleep for fifty-five minutes
I was moving around on the sofa
I couldn't breathe properly
I could see my hand on the yellow cushion
When I had moved
My hand was still on the yellow cushion
Curled, not a complete fist, but a curled hand
I was screaming for help, but no one heard me
I couldn't breathe properly
It was happening all over again

I finally opened my eyes
This time I opened them for real
Even though I had opened them already
Or so I thought
The first thing I looked at was my hand
And it was on the yellow cushion
In an almost fist
Now my sofa is grey
Grey, Yellow, Grey Yellow
What is happening

NIGHTMARES

I can hardly keep my eyes open
I'm scared to go back to sleep
Am I awake
Or am I asleep?
ZS Argenio
Written early hours of the morning, upon waking from sleep paralysis.

'Close My Eyes'

I close my eyes
To rest my peace
Except when I do
You do not cease

I twist and turn
And open my eyes
For frightful comes
It's you; I recognise

Awake, I will be
Till I know your gone
Then I try again
And sleep till dawn
By ZS Argenio

CHAPTER 6

Sickness

To feel positive has got to be the gateway to better well-being. I don't know your situation. I can only hope that, as the reader, your health is in top form. If it isn't and you are struggling physically or mentally, know that you can find many gateways online. Do your research. Please ask someone you trust to help you if you are struggling. There is no shame in asking for help and assistance.

Not all disabilities and poor health are visible. When you have been out and about, maybe you have seen someone park in a disabled car park. Did you also see them get up and walk perfectly out of their car? Did you wonder to yourself or maybe judge a little? You didn't see and won't know why they have that disabled badge. It isn't your place to judge, so maybe stop and think of life's struggles; we are all tested, some of us more than others.

I got sick a few years ago; I remember the day as clearly as anything. The Sunday before was like any other; only my leg started feeling very painful; I put up with it until Monday morning when I drove myself to the Drs. After that, for a while, things went downhill; I needed care and assistance in the hospital and when I was discharged after about two weeks. My mind was about to go on a downhill journey; I couldn't see a way out. I needed to put the work into myself and gain more self-control, except I didn't know how.

Sometimes I think when we are given a diagnosis, our mind somehow changes course. It did for me, anyway.

I did what I did best and eventually wrote about it. I have written poetry for others who also suffer physically or mentally from their health. I have also helped cares ad family members with gift poetry for someone who needs cheering up.

In the chapter I have included, 'Memory,' I worked alongside a wonderful woman who wanted me to write something for her mother. Bringing memories alive was important, so I incorporated some she had shared with me into the poem.

'Autoimmune'

Sorry if you think I'm a pain; I don't mean to be
Sometimes my body is a little mean to me
I try hard to do all my breathing
Only my urine controls my being
This diagnosis will never stop me from getting better
Or writing poetry and a beautiful letter
It just means that sometimes I'm off my feet for a little while
I always greet you with the biggest smile
I am optimistic; any day, I will be cured
For all this makes me very bored
I will bind it and sweat it, and in the sauna, I will go
For everyone, especially you, I will show,
That the metals and mould
It will turn bitter and cold
They will come out of my body with no hold
My skin will feel smooth. My legs won't be drunk
My mind will feel free instead of sunk
My tummy will not be bloated
Not forever in bed
I will be empty of autoimmune
From evening to morning through to noon.
Every day I will be fresh

Let me give you a guess
The day will come; it will be a new me
From my body withdrawn, the autoimmunity free
ZS Argenio

'Memory,'

I know you, but you don't know me
I see you, but you can't see me
I hold on to every bit of memory
If I could have one wish, I would set you free.

It hit me hard, but you harder
Days became dark, but for you, darker
Nights became long, but for you, longer
For us both, I promise to become stronger

As my hands shake, I see you shake even more
In your eyes, memories lost from before
I will hold you close; we will walk
I will listen on repeat as you talk

We will go back in time together
A sweet place in your mind, you remain forever
You mesmerise me with the beautiful stories you share
I'm listening, mum, with duty, love and care

You ask me, "did you enjoy the helicopter ride?"
I search my memory for the kindest answer; I must find
Now, what you don't see

Is that I am entering into your reality

You are so beautiful, yet very frail
Another remote memory, you're learning braille
You say for hours learning, to write me a letter
I was away at school. You knew it would make me feel better

You bring the past alive, just like a fairy-tale
Aboard another memory, we set sail
I love this one; you're teaching me to walk
You guide me through with your gentle talk.

"Stand your feet on top of mine,"
You say as you hold my hands and walk from behind
Now it's my turn; I will shelter you from the storm
I promise to keep you safe and warm

I will always hold your hand as you did mine
Forever my beautiful mum
You make my heart forever shine.
ZS Argenio
Written for a wonderful lady, Deborah, for her beautiful mum, who sadly suffers from a form of Dementia.

'When It Is Hard'

Sometimes I find it hard
Especially when I feel not good enough
I look around for some inspiration
I'm determined, like-minded and tough

Sometimes it's really difficult
Especially to get motivation
So, I have to remind myself
That writing is my passion

Sometimes my workload is heavy
Especially with many projects
Then I remind myself
It's ok to be a bit complex

So, I rearrange my work to suit
That's how I deal with it
I then get on and type, type, type
While in my comfy chair, I sit
ZS Argenio

"I PRAY TO GOD EVERY NIGHT, NOT BECAUSE HE WILL ANSWER THEM, BUT BECAUSE HE WILL LISTEN WITHOUT JUDGEMENT."

'Anxiety'

Mind racing, anxiety is in full swing
I stopped listening
I can't bear it
I won't accept it

Take it away, please
Fight Flight or freeze
I'm in it all
Don't let me fall
ZS Argenio.
Written for a stranger.

> **"A SMILE TO A STRANGER CHANGES THEIR WHOLE DAY, SO BE THAT DIFFERENCE AND SMILE."**
>
> ZS Argenio

'My Diagnosis'

Waking up and going to work was amazing
I would walk there too, and to myself, I'd sing
I buzz myself through the gate
And get ready for the kids, and hope I wasn't late
For playtime was fun
Hop, skip and jump
Sometimes we would learn a dance
I used to encourage the kids to take a chance
Lots of fun they would have every day
I, too, enjoyed my job. 'I love it' to myself, I'd say

Until one day, my life was about to change
The children's group I would need to rearrange
For I woke that day with a sore leg
I couldn't quite feel it; I'll never forget
Still, I went to work to do my skipping with the kids
My shoes I had to remove, for the feeling was hit and miss

I packed up early on that day
I told the kids to go home and play
I told the parents I'd see them next week
Little did I know, too soon, I would speak

I came home as usual to cook the kid's dinner
opened my wine, tasted lush; what a winner
The evening approached, then the night
My leg was burning in pain and felt tight
I waited for the morning to come
I went to the Drs and told them my leg was numb
"Go home and rest"
The Dr said
Call 999
If the numbness was to spread

So, home I drove, with a little thought
What if a weird virus I had caught
I called my boss and told them I wouldn't be in
Little did I know the change was about to begin

After that, an ambulance came
"We think it's a stroke, for its presenting the same"
By this time, I couldn't move either leg
The pain was unbearable, "help me" id beg

I got to the hospital by eleven AM that morning
I had an MRI then came the warning
"We need to do a 'lumbar puncture' just to see"
"What's going on inside your body, and what could it be"

SICKNESS

Then after that, the dreaded words came out
'YOU HAVE MULTIPLE SCLEROSIS

I just wanted to scream and shout
In twenty-four hours, I'd lost the ability to walk
Now I had lost the ability to talk
As well as lost some of my motor skills
"Will this be fixed with lots of pills"
"NO!"

I felt so confused and so alone
But I tried my hardest not to moan
I got worse and worse; I even forgot my kids
This wasn't something that could be easily fixed

My older girls would visit me
I thought one was my mum; she kindly just humoured me
You see, now I'd lost a big part of my memory
Every day without fail
My girls would visit, even though I was frail

I can now remember an unfortunate day
where the nurses had to send my kids away
As I had got too sick to see anyone

I was getting worse; this was not fun
I had to wear these dark glasses to block out the light
It was now all too much; I knew I must fight

Two weeks passed, and I desperately wanted to go home
I needed to be with my family, for in the hospital, I felt so alone
I knew now that I had to learn to walk
And I needed to find my words so I could talk
With my support worker and determination
I get to go home and build new foundations

The fantastic support worker had put things in place
She then took me home; I remember all the kid's faces
All six were so happy to see me
A bed in the living room they had made me

A new journey would begin for us all
I would never give up if I should fall
I would learn to become independent
And not dwell on the MS diagnosis as resentment
With the love and support of my family
I would, again, start to be whole and learn a new me
ZS Argenio

CHAPTER 7

Family

I had dreams of being a mother from a young age; I remember having this baby doll when I was very young, and oh, how I loved her so much; she really was my everything, I would lay her clothes on a blanket in the summer months out the front, and there I would play for ages, or at least until my mum called me in for tea. I don't think I was a problematic child, just your average kid. I liked my bike too. It was my favourite colour, Pink.

Not all of us have a ten-year plan when we are young or know what we will do when we are older. I knew one thing I wanted to do when I was older; I wasn't sure how I would execute it or even if I would ever marry, but one obvious thing was that I would start my family, and I did.

I am so blessed to have four daughters, two sons and five grandchildren and counting. I also have my wonderful soul mate.

Family, to me, is everything, as you will see from the poetry I have written for my family.

In the chapter, I have included a couple of pieces of my work which I have written for other families. When asked to write for someone else, it brings me so much joy, especially from a child to a parent or caregiver.

'My Brother'

Moving to a new place was like entering a new season
It could have been cold or hot, but never was I given a reason
Even though my behaviour played a massive part
Still, I wouldn't say I liked the fresh starts
I would always leave an unpacked bag
In case I wanted to run away from a constant nag
Or something else, which would mean id need to escape
I was hoping that this place would be great

I won't go into detail as I'm writing this in my family chapter
So, I'll stick to all the positive factors.

I was out there again one day; I'd been dropped off
At the same usual spot, this time freezing, with a cough
Trying to pull myself together, brushing away
All the dirt, grime and hay
There you were again, staring through the pub window
I knew you would come over, warm me up like my softest pillow
You had this way that made me feel safe and warm
A brother and sister bond had already formed

You promised to look after me and took me under your wing
You would surprise me with all the new clothes you would bring
You did rather spoil me, especially with love and care
Fast forward a bit older, you would take me to the fair
All the girls loved you, especially your blonde curtains
I was so proud of you; you were my brother, and that was certain

Let us fast forward a little bit more
I had moved again; these foster parents were lovely; that's for sure
You pulled up one day to bring me a gift
I was more interested in getting a lift
In your awesome BMW, it was silver or blue
I had to wait, as again you had spoilt me with something new
Two rabbits and a hutch; I named them Bubbles and Squeaks
I was so grateful and happy for weeks and weeks
Then one day, I went out of the back to my rabbits
I opened the hutch to pick them up; it was a habit
I was not expecting to see what I saw
There were no longer two rabbits: so many more

FAMILY

Little tiny pink things inside a pile of fur
But how could this be? You told me they were two her's
That means a boy and a girl
What the hell..!

Let's fast forward once again
Our bond had grown over the years
You were always there wiping my tears
Didn't matter if they were happy or sad
You were there, a constant I always had
A bond we had like no other
And now you were a loving father
And I, a loving mother
We even ended up living on the same street
Together with the kids, we would meet
New memories we would make
Even today, I love them; they're great

I want you to know how much I appreciate you
And all of the beautiful things you do
I know we've had ups and downs, even some years apart
But you are always that one person so close to my heart
You, dear brother, my favourite person
You have taught me so much, always to keep learning

I'm so glad across me you stumbled
Without you, brother, my world would have crumbled
Thank you for always being my big brother
ZS Argenio
Written for a special person in my life. While I understand that blood makes you related. This man became my brother not by blood but by the power of true hearts.

'Foster parents'

It takes dedication, hard work and love
To look after someone else's child
That is exactly what you did for me
Even though I was extremely wild

I will always be grateful to you both
For never giving up on me
Even though I was so challenging
Your love, it set me free.
ZS Argenio

"YOU ONLY GET ONE MUM, EVERYTHING THAT SHE TELLS YOU, SHE DOES SO BECAUSE SHE LOVES YOU. YOUR MUM MAY NOT ALWAYS GET IT RIGHT, BUT SHE LOVES YOU. JUST REMEMBER THAT NO MATTER HOW OLD YOU ARE YOU WILL ALWAYS BE HER BABY.
LOVE HER AND TREAT HER LIKE A QUEEN.
IF YOU FALL OUT, TAKE THE TIME TO MAKE-UP.
I LOVE MY MUM; I WILL ALWAYS LOVE MY MUM."

ZS Argenio

'To My Sister,'

My sister and I love playing in the sand
Turning in circles, holding each other's hands
The wind blows strong
In our faces, we feel it as we walk along
Sometimes it blows me over
It makes my sister laugh, big poser
We run together. She never leaves me behind
We are laughing because we know what's on each other's mind
Mischief, of course, as we are only one and three
In the water, jumping each wave, that's where we want to be
Only grandma says, 'It's too cold for that,'
As she puts on our woolly hats
So instead, we sit in the sand and pick out rocks
We will play and stack them like blocks
Then up again, on the beach, let's run
I love being with my sister; we have so much fun
Sometimes we fight, but I don't know why
I'm sorry if I ever make you cry

You're my best friend, Amaia-Rain,
Can we play at the beach again?
ZS Argenio
Written for my granddaughters, Aiva to Amaia.

"BLOOD IS NOT THE ONLY REASON YOU ARE FAMILY
YOU ARE FAMILY BECAUSE YOU HAVE A HEART BIG ENOUGH TO LOVE."

ZS Argenio

'Dear Son,'

I know some days you feel overwhelmed or insecure
And asking for help is difficult, I'm sure
I wish your silent cries no more
No looking behind, as you have before

It won't be easy; I'm not going to lie
But this is something you must try
Be the person you really want to be
Align with your heart, let your mind agree
There's a whole world with no limit on time
Take this moment to stand and shine

When you feel scared
Or unprepared
Take a moment, breathe; it's ok,
For its ok, not be ok

You are on a journey
And there is so much to see
Experience Life
Be all you ever inspire to be
You've got this, a new beginning
Allow your heart to start singing

FAMILY

You will look back one day
To yourself, you will say
I did it
I'm doing it
I love you, son.

ZS Argenio
Written for a lovely lady, Sharon (for her son)

'Grandma's Roasties'

My hands prepare the dinner
While my mind prepares for the day
I can't wait to see you all
And listen to what you say

I glistened the roasties with glaze
Your favourite Sunday dinner
Not too many veggies
But the roasties are most definitely a winner

Bring yourself and my grandkids too
For a happy, glorious Sunday
Let's make brand-new memories
Like we do every day

So, a happy new Sunday, kids
Be sure to eat your dinner
For grandma's roasties are the best
Winner, winner, chicken dinner
ZS Argenio
Written for my family, for every Sunday that we are blessed to get together.

'My Grandkids,'

The kids come running through the door
Pitta, Pitta, of their feet on the floor
Out come the toys
With lots of noise
With giggles and laughter
The cuddles come after
With all the noise and sounds
I love having my grandkids around
ZS Argenio
Written for my grandchildren., and every blessed grandparent/caregiver out there.

'Mummy'

Thank you for all the things you do for me.

I like it when I wake in the morning
And into your room, I run
Big giant kisses you give me
Today is going to be fun

I like it when we go out to eat
And in a mess, I get
'Silly sausage', you say to me
Then ice cream you go and fetch.

I like it when we do 'hide and seek'
Or you take me to the park
My favourite time with you is play
And cuddles in the dark.

I like it when you hold my hand
Your never far away
You give me so many cuddles
you do this every day

FAMILY

I like it when you read me stories
And tuck me in my bed
You are my favourite person
I'll always rather be with you instead

Thank you for being my mummy
And my very special friend
I can't wait for tomorrow
T do it all again

I love you, mummy
ZS Argenio
Written for Jade (from her beautiful little boy)

'Spontaneous Moments'

Little eyes looking up at us both
Speaking in a language of love
'Can we go outside today?'
You say, looking at us above

We go on a journey
Through natures desire
Footsteps crisp in the leaves
Let us sit here for a while

All around, you see birds flying
And the wind brushing the grass
The smell of autumn in the air
And birds fly fast

'Look up,' I say
'Look over there'
You point your little fingers
and begin to stare

For along came a Robin
Perched on a branch
Staring right back at you all
In nature, taking a chance

In that moment
You watched in utter pleasure
You gave Robin a great big smile
A picture I took, what a treasure!
ZS Argenio.
Written for my grandchildren. Our day out in a nature reserve.

'Grandchildren A Blessing'

I love my grandbabies
From the bottom of my heart
They bring me so much joy
And have from the very start

They make my heart smile
And fill me with laughter
They greet me with a hug
And love me forever after.

They fill the house with love
As well as toys galore
They leave crumbs at their feet
And dance across the floor

They love playing with my guitar
And filling the house with noise
Avia, Amaia, and Rosie
As well as both my boys

FAMILY

They love to give giant kisses
And lots of cuddles too
Especially PJ and Bhodi
They are the smallest two

With outside playtime
Comes splashing in the puddles
They love our forest schools
And exciting games and puzzles

When it's time for them to leave
I whisper in their ear
Grandma and Nonna love you
All around are smiles and cheer
We love our grandbabies.
ZS Argenio
Written for my grandchildren.

'How Many'

First child Second child
Then there comes a Third
How many children
Will God send me to earth?

Fourth child Fifth child
Then there comes a sixth
My perfect family
A graceful mix

Not forgetting the loving angels
That came in between
They grow their beautiful flying wings
To God, they were Kings and Queens
ZS Argenio
Written for all my dear children.

'My Babies'

I wanted a large family
A love beyond existence
Protection I'll give forever
I promise never to be distant

The love that binds our family
It is the greatest gift of all
And being a mum to six
I will be nothing without you all
ZS Argenio
Written for all my dear children.

CHAPTER 8

Trauma

(TRIGGER WARNING FOR ALL THIS CHAPTER)

Some say a book should never start with 'Once Upon A Time' and end with 'Happily ever after.' I always wonder to myself why? Through all the courses I have taken on creative writing, unless you are writing a children's storybook that often starts with such a title and ends with 'happily ever after,' there are many reasons to refrain from such a title, as much as there is to start with your 'Once Upon A times' There is a reason I want to start with such a title because it was indeed just once upon a time then I would like to follow with, in a faraway land, only the distant land was in my head. You will read it yourself and create your own picture story for these poems as you are my audience, and no two people read any poem the same; you will relate in your way, or you may not relate at all.

I chose the end for myself; I decided you did not win; you would no longer control my thought pattern, and I would not be in your control anymore, even though you had been a 'once upon a time, you hadn't been a 'happily ever after' for you did leave me to seep these wounds and heal on my own as did the people I thought I could trust! I used to believe that the day would never come when I would stop thinking about it or wonder how I could have changed that whole day from when I woke up to when I went to play outside. As I grew older, I had already been through so much more, so I always went back to a particular day and blamed myself. That day was the reason for the weeks, months, and years that were to come. That day was the reason for every negative choice I made. That day would be the reason I misbehaved so severely as a child.

Moments like picture images would go through my head, and sometimes they would surface daily, on what I could have done differently; Except I was a child, and I had no control, although I learnt to take accountability for my actions later in life.

When we are subjected to trauma as a youngster, if it's not dealt with at the time, it can show up in our behaviours later in life. We think we have masked it, almost hidden it, and sometimes ignorance is bliss, but it will always have a way to surface.

I am a firm believer in forgiveness. I chose to practise forgiveness to feel free of hurt, anger or pain. I understand that it can be tough to overlook for any reason, and some people find it hard to forgive another or don't forgive at all. Not forgiving someone is a personal choice. I've decided to forgive in many situations, not just people, but I have also needed to forgive myself.

I received a phone call out of the blue, asking me if I had seen the news. I did not know what this person was referring to. After a brief conversation, my head went into overdrive. I said I was fine and wouldn't overthink it; after all, many years had already passed, so why would I give it a second thought? Only that was a lie; the only thing I could think of was the knock on the door. Then after that, flashbacks. I had already suffered in silence with my mental health, and even after the mental health services tried to help me, I never felt whole; there was always something missing. One way to explain the feeling was that a part of me wasn't quite joined together.

I did what I always do best, and I wrote so much poetry; it has always helped me to get things out, it is like a slight relief to get it on paper. Some of this writing is very graphic, but it's my way of sharing my truths and healing.

TRAUMA

(Extreme Trigger Warning-Graphic)
'It's Happened Before,'

The pain is too much to bear
As in my eyes, I look, and I stare
All I see is one face, then another
All faces on top of me, as underneath I smother
I can't see for winds; they breathe so violently
So, I just lay here frightened, silently
No thought in my mind, Can I bear
Or reaching with fright, ever do I dare
one after another, not even decisively
'Why now? As an adult, I should have known, not surprisingly!
IT HAPPENED BEFORE
A room so blank a wall and a mattress
Just before this, the heat of glass, smoked, then passed around like a waitress
Only takes one to 'crack' being the ultimate word
'Slut' in turns 'room' 'let's go' is all I heard
A dirty mattress lay on the floor
A loud bang from the slam of the door
My breasts touched and squeezed through my clothes; it hurt

Hands, lots of them, pulling at my legs from under my skirt
His trousers undone, in my mouth, down my throat
Hair pulled by another, as I hear them gloat
All over my skin, turned over, hands held down
In one would go, then another, I'm going to drown
ITS HAPPENED BEFORE
I blank out, do not cry, dismiss myself
In mind, at least, I try to be someone else
Faces everywhere, one hand on them, other on me
In my head, I'm running; I'm free
'Dirty whore, get dressed,'
No time for crying; I try to look my best
Looking around this dirty room, my mind a wander
What's just happened? My mind's a thunder
Funny; one suggests putting me on the bus
They need me gone now. What's the rush?
He walks me to the bus stop, asks why I'm a slag
And to all them a free giving shag
He even pays for my ticket, gives them the fair and off I go
I sit on the bus in my seat and wonder
Can anyone see? Does anyone know?
IT HAPPENED BEFORE!
ZS Argenio

"THE DAY WILL BEGIN WHEN YOU ARE READY, SO WHEN YOU ARE READY, LET THE DAY BEGIN."

ZS Argenio

'Solitude'

I found a way
A way through
Where no one can see me
Not even you
When I get there
I sit inside
Where no one's there
Not even behind
I will pull and tug
Everything out
Of course, now there is no one about
Tears down my face
They always fall
As nothing, no one can see
What I feel at all
Out of mind
Burn to cook
As no one is here to
Of course, look
It's racing a strategy of time
For I see you
Yet there is NO crime
My thoughts you took over

TRAUMA

A life you lead
As for you
It was all in good stead
To me, a burden lived over and over
Not a single person believed
Maybe they do now that you are lowered
You left me to seep these wounds
To then heal
As you're not here now
You're not real
For me, it was done
For you not won
I'll always behold
As of right as can be
Of course
You can't see me
Where are you?
Beneath the soil?
You still have a way
To make my blood boil
Please leave me alone
For you're gone
I know what you did
Was WRONG!
ZS Argenio

'The Street'

Young, naïve, scared, and alone,
One thing you dare NOT do is moan.
'Take it, bitch, you dirty whore,'
You hear that said so much; it becomes a chore!
'Hello my love, get in, hurry. How much?'
Their hands are all over you, not one piece of you they can't touch!

'Hey, you two names, please? go now before I get you.'
another spot you go, not far from the men
Not them again!

'Hey, isn't it....? Get in; I'm going to help you,'
'Sign this so they know why you're in my car.'
The thought of being saved instead of taken afar!
Silly expectations. It was about getting in his car
A false sense of security
From the man of authority!

Taken to remote locations, hay stakes hurting you
Rougher each time he betrays you
As you're told exactly what to do

TRAUMA

One night as you lay in your bed
It's time to rest
Only God gives you yet another test

The buzzer to your room goes off
You answer, clearing your throat with a cough
'Come down; labour has started,'
To the voice, you are moulded
'Hurry, get in.' behind you, the car door shuts!
The danger you feel
This can't be real.

To Heath, a memory that won't forget!
'Need to drop something off,'
Yeah. I bet!
From the driver's seat to the boot
Now it's time to run
Woodland and a road
What if in hand he has a gun?

You know, to stay in the seat
 Now a blade pressed against your neck
You feel the heat
Survival mode kicks in
Begging for mercy, you begin.

'Give me one reason I don't kill you now?'
You hear him say, to him, you must bow
"What about your wife?"
That's all you could think while up against a knife
Salvation through questions
Scared of his words, a dirty infection
Danger from the man on the street
Now you beg for mercy at his feet

In the woodland, you're both alone
Shaken, for scared to the bone!
You must now play along
But for how long?
It's him I must fulfil
It's better than being killed

He then takes me back as if nothing happened!
ZS Argenio

'Negative,'

How negative do you feel?
Your heart appalled
And not to steal.

Blanked from warmth
Only cold inside
Not nothing within
You will find!

A sunken hole
That cannot be filled
Instead, I think
inside it's killed.

Any emotion
That may surface
Blank expression
Has its purpose!

Nothing can see
The spark is blown
All good is rotten
It's all you've known!

Unsettled
A feeling of neglect
A point
You can't re-select!

No un-doing
Flow so sad
Yet taking the fear
Good to bad!

No sorrow shows
Just an empty shell
Of what once stood
Has now fell!

Pour over the melody of silence

How negative do you feel?
Your heart appalled
And not to steal!
ZS Argenio

> **"IT IS OK; THERE IS ALWAYS TOMORROW."**
>
> ZS Argenio

'Left To Fall'

Smudged between the surface
Everything is broken
Time does not fix
Left fallen.

Sadness left behind
No strength to rekindle
Everything went long ago
Left to fall.

Alone, alone, alone
Just a book as a friend
For there never was anyone
So, no need to pretend.

Alone in thought
Alone in this world
Alone with thought
Alone in this world.
ZS Argenio.

TRAUMA

'Your Car'

When I close my eyes
All I see is you
The tattoo on your face
And the thing you made me do

I will never understand
Why I got into your car
I knew it was going to be bad
And I knew you would take me far

You Went to the trunk of your car
And told me to be still
I wanted to run
It was me you wanted to kill

I decided to stay sitting
In the passenger side seat
And when you got back in
A knife you had me greet

You held it to my throat
And ask me why you should not
I spoke with politeness
My head has never forgot

I wondered if I should scream
Or give out a shout
But no one would hear me
The woods, no one about

I felt the blade was cold
Yet your hand was so warm
I was scared to the bone
How did I get into this storm?

I spoke my words kindly
And listened to what you said
Even though I was shaking
I befriended you instead

I did not want to die
By your hands and your knife
I was just a kid
And I had my whole life

TRAUMA

I made a deal with you
God was on my side
You drove me back to the hostel
And sex was my tour guide
ZS Argenio

'Face'

Playing in the garden
Picking at the flowers
Running in the grass
I'm there for hours

It's time to go in
A bath you had run
Something's not right
It is no longer fun

I can't see your face
I don't know who you are
I know you're there
And can smell a cigar

I'm older now
And I still can't see your face
So, I don't know who you are
You're a sick disgrace
ZS Argenio

'Daydream'

Mind is known to wander
It's a safe space for me
I look into the distance
But there is nothing to see

You try and pull me out
Telling me I'm in a daydream
I wish I could tell you why
Only the wounded head will scream

Just know it's my safe space
Where not nothing can hurt
I don't mean any harm
I'm just digging in the dirt

It's not like it's paradise
Or sunset with the beach
It's just a safe place
Where I can get some sleep
ZS Argenio

'Go Away'

You travel through my skin and bones
Every waking hour
I can't get you off me
Not even when I shower

You're gone for good
Why doesn't my brain see that
I'll never understand
I guess that's where I'm at

You think you took it all from me
But I'm telling you that you didn't
You are now under the ground
Good riddance
ZS Argenio

'Prostitute.'

I'll see you in my dreams tonight
Underneath that bright red light
I'll watch you get into those cars
And see you gaze upon the stars
Hand to hand goes all the money
Thinking that it's very funny
Then off he drops you on that street
Which streets that Ber Street
From me (Written in 1994)

CHAPTER 9

letters.

(TRIGGER WARNING THROUGH THIS CHAPTER)

Letters to yourself or others are an excellent form of communication; and a way to express how one is feeling. Sometimes, words in a letter can speak more than words we try to talk out loud.

I decided to call this chapter 'letters' for it was many a letter that I had written for myself, a way to reflect and journal my thoughts and feelings. As you have seen over and over in this book, poetry has been a lifeline for me. I have been in some fucked up situations, whether I have put myself there or not. It's been so fucked up that I can't see the sun for the clouds. This has been my state of mind on so many occasions.

From good to bad, positive to negative, journaling and poetry is my lifeline.

'Dear Me,'

To you, as a child
Innocent, free, and wild
All you wanted was healthy love and kindness
That's ok to want
As you stand there looking gaunt
Writing in your pretty font
Playing your music
Thinking of your cupid
It's not stupid
It's your acoustic
You're playing your confusion
Like it's an illusion
Of your conclusion
Of what's happening all around you
You feel like a dog in a zoo
Trying to break through
You run, lose a shoe
Like a door without a screw
It's stuck like glue
Won't snap like bamboo
You, your brave from those who enslave you
Like a heatwave
Enclosed small like a microwave

LETTERS.

No wonder why you misbehave
Just remember your brave
You hid in the depths of your mind
Still being kind
While outlined and still blind
As your tiny mind
Again assigned
Never declined
For your fear was very clear
Always so near
Like you were someone's career
Feeding them their beer
Whilst you always missed your school year!
Please know
Although you felt you must do as those desire
So, you didn't expire
All the time, you wish for a wildfire,
To miss the crossfire
To not cause panic and go haywire
You would just lay and give a stare
As that was all that was there
Because you were scared!
I can only tell you that being scared was OK
You did what you did to survive
Going into overdrive

Knowing no better
As you sat writing your letter
Making a treasure map
Hoping you don't get a slap
As you recap the hidden gap
Between you and the mousetrap
A mouse you saved
While being enslaved
As you wave goodbye to your mum
Feeling numb
Not knowing the outcome
While sitting carelessly chewing gum
That this was now you all alone
You would never moan
While being on the phone
Scared to the bone
In your safe zone
Your beautiful imagination
Throughout all duration
Of all flirtations
As your heart gave palpitations
While you wish for salvation
A beautiful imagination
Of all your creations
As your once child, look at you now

LETTERS.

All grown loved, and all fears conquered,
With your family in tow
Only love do they know
Nothing is dearer than the one thing you always wanted
Was stability
Full of tranquillity
No humility
Just great ability
And hostility
As this life is now, love, kindness and courage
No discourage
Only encouraging each other
Remember you as a child
Some your fault
But no rape or sexual assault
You were just a child
That was styled
And made wild.
If only in the future at the time; you could see
A happy, positive person you'd be
You fill all lives with beautiful colours
Giving your children sisters and brothers
From a victim
You became a survivor
A great provider

As well as an adviser
Of pure greatness and love
In this
You become a writer
ZS Argenio

'Fight For Freedom,'

Finding you can be challenging. Tell me, where do you start?
In some most uncertain fears, with yourself especially, can you part?
It can feel like cutting all your moments in half
As your history is part of you, some are sad but don't forget the laughs
The point is, make that journey, start now, head up high, and walk your path
Make it your discovery of shaping your mind that sometimes feels torn in half
Rid yourself of negative thoughts, instead fill with courage and all things positive
I understand this can be hard. Allow it to be your motive
You can do it; think 'victim'. How do you feel?
Lost? Fearful? Abandoned trust? Like it's all gone, almost as if it's still so real?
Now try hard, think 'Survivor' go on, make it personal
How do you feel? It's not just a word; find that courage and start your own journal
Write all your thoughts of today, not yesterday

Then in time, as you write, you will reflect, and the word 'Victim' will slowly fade away
The thought that once you were someone's prized possession
Will now be your gain, a journal of your bright confessions
Please keep it in sight, look around, and your safe, nice clean, fresh air
It's you; your thought process changes, you're riding your anger and despair
I know you can do this 'A great survivor', feel it and own it
As you chop down these limp memories bit by bit
Try now and reflect; try looking at your beauty in the mirror
Everything you ever wanted to see will now be so much clearer
Coming from a victim to a survivor means you can now look ahead
Instead of being behind, the sadness is stopping; you don't feel so alone, you're not
Laid procrastinating in bed
You now know nothing is misled
Your feelings are valid as you learn to look straight ahead

LETTERS.

You're on this journey to become a survivor
Now you are your most excellent adviser
Ask yourself again, how do you feel? Deep breath, now smile
This wasn't something you could do comfortably as a child
Only you can take stead and broaden your mind
As in your heart, on your new journey, you're still you, still loving and kind.
This means you're beating it; you're feeling less and less a victim
With this new outlook, you can start living you can smile with all hope and dignity
You will feel comfortable helping others, offering now your empathy
Showing them beliefs and sympathy
Your brain so fresh, awakened feels so clean
The best version of you inside you have ever felt and seen
Nothing now will intervene; you won't let anything get in between
The new you.... look in the mirror and love the new you
No longer are you hidden in the depths of fear
For now, a survivor. Everything else seems crystal clear

Keep smiling and, importantly, keep writing in your journal
For this new wisdom that, my dear, is eternal
Now, from a victim to a survivor, there is one thing you can guarantee
No longer will you look over your shoulder; for now, there's nothing to see
From all your past to future, remembering and living in the present
That all you were wasn't just a labelled lesson,
It was something that would make you, in oneself, a survivor.
You are a blessing.
ZS Argenio

'Searching'

One day you are searching for something you realise you have been searching
For your whole life. What is it, you may ask? Let me tell you.

From birth to mother, will never feel like no other
Being told all the time, 'The reflection is all mine'
Yet you come from drugs and crime to clean in no time
Still finding your mind. In front of the wall, you still climb.
Still battling with your self-confidence, this, you know to be true
Because this is you
Everything is a daze, stuck in time
You're still hoping to shine
This is something you will find
If you stop going backwards and looking behind
Else you will miss your stop, for you will be blind!
One thing you're not is never unkind
You need to come out of a harmful process in your mind
Then and only then will you see a tiny glimpse of what it is you're searching for
Even if you must visit right to the core

As remember, not every day the same old chore of faking that smile,
Because all the while
Mind creates its system of negative files
Ones you want gone!
Try positive thinking,
I promise within your boundaries of thought
It will all be new, self-taught
You will have the ability to remove your mask. It's been on for years
Then you can show real emotion and even happy tears
No longer will you feel empty with no clue
For you will learn positively what to do
You already love your children with honour and protection,
You're not frightened to feel with great emotion and affection
A mother-child bond you have will never be like no other
For this a promise, you made the minute you became a mother
Maybe what you are searching for you have already found
For the child, you love unconditionally, to this forever bound!

LETTERS.

A gift from the good lord himself, beauty and strength
So in mind, you can resolve great things at such length
Give away the darkness of sad history; now let it be
Forever now an unsolved mystery
God has always listened every time you pray,
He takes your sorrow and pain away
He helps you believe that a good mother, you will be
Taught in your mind this love is here to stay!
What you are searching for is in front of you
You may not always know the answer or what to do
But you sure know how to love and protect
Even if you look back to reflect
The decisions you made, the life you took
Is the reason you're here, to write this book
So go ahead, look, and tell me what you see.
Your own beautiful little family.
Your creations, your new life, this beautiful chance
You may have searched, no need, for now, an extraordinary circumstance
That is filling you full of smiles and joy of precious, so deep
A mountain of laughter, right here, your family to keep
A beautiful family, the one you have created
You will never become separated.
Believe in yourself, for the storm is over

Positive from now, let go of the anger
The clouds aside, the sunshine is through
You searched, look, it's still you!
ZS Argenio

'In a Kingdom'

In a kingdom far away, I dream of everything kind!
As I put pen to paper, I find words hard to find
I open my eyes and remember; the dream was not reality
Not everything is as we will see!
A heart so heavy filled solely with pain
Reaching out, what do I seek? What do I gain?
I tried hard not to take things to heart
But I always have from the very start
As early as mind can but feel pain and sorrow
Remembering my cries and hoping for a better tomorrow
I waited, helped, protected from the cruellest
Only me, they would see a subject to test!
A burden carried for such a long time
When is my time to shine?
So as pen-to-paper words hard to find
In a kingdom, I dream everything so kind
Until eyes open, and know that's not to be
Because in this reality, nothing is as you see
What if power we had so clear to change
Every choice and turn, we could rearrange
The power of the universe taken hold so tight

That in life, it was no longer fight or flight
Everything from our being of insecurities
Changed to colours, no more impurities
To be able to look around
Here laughter and all-natural sound
No teardrops, from eye to cheek
Not nothing ever harmful in eyes reach
Start to build, try hard.
As I write this poem on a layer of card
We can all wish for great beginnings
On the road, il go for beautiful sightseeing
No hold over, no burden to carry, I'll let go
No negative energy, I will say no
Though, as I say, words are hard to find
In a kingdom, I dream so precious and kind
Till I open my eyes, there I will find
It's everywhere, awake, asleep; look behind
Wishful thinking to create such kindness
As I sit and write, I'm sat so still in blindness
ZS Argenio

'Can you See Me'

Can you see me?
Can you see me?
I'm here in every breath you hold
Can you see me?
Can you see me?
I'm in you, a heart that cannot fold
Can you see me?

I came to you in your dreams of night
Not ever knowing
The path I was showing
was it love?
Is it love?
It's like the clouds are flowing
Every day I'm glowing
Growing
But in heart, its pain
Now the clouds are filled with rain.

Can you see me?
Can you see me?
I'm here in every breath you hold
Can you see me?

Can you see me?
I'm in you, a heart that cannot fold
Can you see me?

I feel like I'm drowning in the rain
not to my pleasure, not to my gain
As only in pain
Slowly I'm feeling
can I be dreaming?
Is this the picture you painted
That I tainted
With broken glass
Nowhere to run, look fast
Nothing to see
Nothing to see.

Can you see me?
Can you see me?
I'm here in every breath you hold
can you see me?
Can you see me?
I'm in you, a heart that cannot fold.
Can you see me?
Can you see me?

LETTERS.

You open your eyes
All you can hear are cries
All around you, filling every space and hole
Slowly suffocating, like the aching of bones
Suffocating
Suffocating
trying to get out, to be able to feel
Not escaping the appeal
Of something so very real

Can you see me? Can you see me?

So let it rain, let it thunder
As everywhere, I wonder
I'm here; I'm here
Do you see me?
Do you see me?
Do you see me?
By ZS Argenio
A song I wrote during the Covid 19 pandemic

'Mine'

You can take, but it won't work
Around the corners, you might lurk
I told you it isn't going
I don't care how much you're showing!
Try hard; I'll say try harder
All you will get is lots of laughter
You will try in the night
But you know I will fight
As I said, it isn't going

What you going to do
wait, so it's like you too?
Nope, not happening
I'll be the one clapping
As all the time I see
There it is, wild and free
So go on, why don't you try?
Because this isn't going to cry!

You know, every day, my whites will show
And you will definitely know
It's my smile
Has been now for a long while

Fight, Fight, Fight
Because they are my pearly whites
A smile you will not undo
Because it's on me, it belongs to me
Not you!
ZS Argenio

'The Fulness of Life I Lead'

At the moment, the life I lead is very difficult
I feel like a complete and utterly shameful piece of crap
Which has been picked up off the ground
And then put it straight back in the bin
Sometimes I get so angry and upset that t I feel suicidal
But what would killing myself do and solve?
Nothing, just the fact that you're running away to leave yourself
But then, when it comes to expressing my feelings, they run away
All I can express mine to is a grotty piece of paper with a poem
Only that's not good at all, but it can't be helped.
I feel like I want to be by myself all the time
Just locked away in one big room with things to do
But no one is around to nag you for doing nothing right
Because they can't
I feel like an odd one out
everyone can laugh and play games
But I can't because of the way I feel; I don't know how to laugh
Yes, that's exactly how I feel
People say that I'm feeling sorry for myself

LETTERS.

Maybe that's the case; I don't know
But what I do know has to be my decision
Thanks for listening
I know your just a bit of paper
I don't care if you listened to me.
From Me (Written in 1992)

'What Do I Do,'

What does one give
When there is nothing left to give
An open heart, I guess
And a desire to live

What does one seek
When there is nothing left to seek
An open door, I guess
Go on and take a peek

What does one do
When one doesn't know what to do
Try something new, I guess
Go on, be you
ZS Argenio

'Feelings'

As each of the long days goes by
I sit here and cry
For there is no one to talk to
And no one to talk to you.

I sit each day in shame.
Thinking it's all one big game
But it's not; I don't listen at all
So, everyone must think I'm one big fool

I must change for everyone's sake
And show them that I'm not just a fake
I can prove that I can be good because I tried
I let nothing take over, not even my pride
Then maybe I won't be so slow
Then hopefully, the future can bring good news
Not just for me
But for everyone.
From me (Written in 1992)

'Dear Toby'

As soon as I saw you, I knew you were smart
And in your eyes, I could see your big heart
That's when I knew our companion you would be
And I knew you would pick me.
From that day on, your journey began
So now it was time to make a plan
So along came your best friend Maisey
With you two together, boy, were you crazy.
You taught Maisey how to dig and run
Under a fence, you would both go, knowing it was fun
For time you did this any chance you got
For the mischief you got up to, I have never forgot.
Remember how you loved to catch a ball
To come back, only your name I would call
And if that ball you would loose
I know another I would choose.
For you, dear Toby, everything was a game
You knew always to be gentle, for you were so beautifully tame.
You loved to be stroked, and the bum dance you would do
It was cute and funny at the same time too.
All the days you would take Maisey and run away

LETTERS.

To me feels only like it was just yesterday
I'm so sorry, Toby, that you started to feel tired
I knew now that sleep was all you desired
For in my heart, I could feel your pain
As did Maisey, even though you would never complain
I sadly wonder if you knew you were dying
It kills me to think that, as my heart keeps crying
I know you felt so loved and cared for
We didn't want you in pain anymore
So, we helped you to cross over the rainbow
Heaven was waiting, dear Toby; off you go
By ZS Argenio
Written for our dear Toby, you will be forever missed.

COMING SOON

'Forbidden Love'
A 1960's LGBTQ+ ROMANCE.
A tale of fate, love and betrayal.
A story that goes deep into the lives of
two women from different cultures.
Does fate bring them together or pull them apart?

Keep up to date, @notjustapoet.

www.ingramcontent.com/pod-product-compliance
Lightning Source LLC
Chambersburg PA
CBHW030259100526
44590CB00012B/445